Introduction to Shapes and Time

This book will help you to introduce your child to some common shapes and words which describe them. It will give opportunities for talking about patterns, including the time patterns in a day. Children show an interest in shapes and time at different ages. Whatever stage your child is at, using this book and watching the DVD together will be an enjoyable and rewarding experience.

The book contains:

- an introduction to lines and shapes

- opportunities for your child to practise talking about size, place and position

- help for your child in beginning to talk about times of the day and night.

Using the pack

The pack contains a DVD of clips taken from the BBC TV programme *Numbertime*. In many of the clips, Little Juan struggles with shapes and time, but the mysterious masked hero El Nombre swings in on his rope to save the day.

Enjoy completing the puzzles and challenges of the pages and watching the DVD. It is better to introduce just one new idea at a time. Don't try to do too much in one go. Enjoy returning to favourite clips and pages as often as you like. This will help to develop confidence and secure earlier learning.

Included in this pack is a poster showing a firework fiesta scene based on characters from the Numbertime programmes. Point out the shapes at the bottom of the poster: a circle, a square, a triangle and a rectangle. See how many of each shape your child can spot hiding in the fiesta picture. Talk about the other shapes you can see: pointed stars, wavy-edged balloons and hats with wide brims. Talk about the different patterns on the clothes of the villagers and the shapes of the food, flags, rockets and moon.

Talking about lines, shapes and position

Lines and shapes

It is very useful to help your child to feel confident in describing lines and shapes. Encourage your child to take a finger for a walk along lines, talking about straight lines, curvy lines and corners. Explore wiggly, loopy lines, lines with zigzags and lines with spiky points.

Use these same kinds of words as you describe flat shapes. Help your child to run a finger around the four sides of a square, or the edge of a round shape. Draw attention to the corners of a rectangle or the curve of a circle.

Talk about objects that your child will be familiar with: 'Can you think of something round which you put food on?' or 'Have you noticed the square tiles in the kitchen?'.

Note: Mathematically speaking, any four-sided flat shape with four right-angled corners is a rectangle, and so a square is a special rectangle with four sides the same length. For this reason, the shape referred to in this book as a rectangle is often called an oblong or an oblong rectangle.

Up and down

Little Juan sings 'Incy Wincy spider'. Join in, moving hands up and down with Incy Wincy. March around the room singing the 'Grand Old Duke of York'. Talk about climbing up and down the stairs. Play the firefighter board game in this book, climbing up the ladders and sliding down the poles.

Over, under, around

Take a teddy for a walk, taking him around furniture, over cushions and under chairs and tables. Play a game in which the tortoise and hare must go over or around the hedge to get to the party.

Around, between, beside

Use mealtimes as an opportunity to talk about where people will sit or where plates should be set. Watch a clip and play a game in which Mama must negotiate her way around holes as she walks to the shop.

Talk about the clips and enjoy spotting Tanto's position!

Playing board games

Several pages in this book take the form of board games where you and your child race along a track. You will find it useful to have an ordinary dice and a few counters, although buttons, pieces of card or small coins could also be used as playing pieces.

Playing track games is an excellent way of helping your child to develop the skills of accurate counting. When moving a counter, it is important to say just one number word for each 'jump'. It can be a good idea to keep a finger on the space where the counting started so that counts can be checked.

Support the language of this book by talking about moving forwards and backwards along the track.

Talking about time

Children are encouraged to talk about the familiar time patterns of day and night, and times of the day. As you work through these pages make links to your own routines, bringing in the key words of morning, afternoon, evening and night.

This book looks at developing the skill of putting events in order. This is called 'sequencing'. The best way for you to help your child with sequencing is to talk about your own shared experiences. Enjoy talking through the events of a special celebration, something funny that happened or an exciting outing. Encourage your child to add to the story by asking: 'Now where did we go first?' or ' What did we do next?'.

Go to page 24 for more top tips.

Looking at lines

Take your finger for a walk along these lines.
Talk about your walk.

Look at all of these funny lines. There is a zigzag,
a wavy line, a wiggly line and a loopy line.

Draw your own lines on some paper.

Run your finger around these shapes. Look for points and curves.

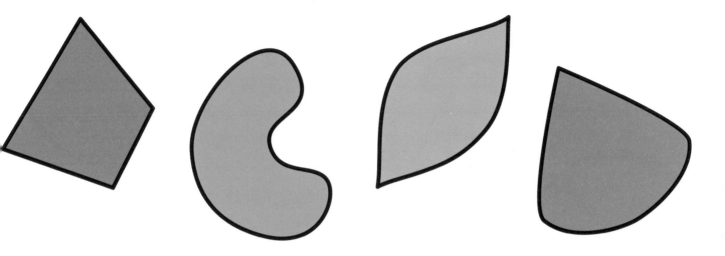

Feel all the corners as you walk along the top of this castle wall.

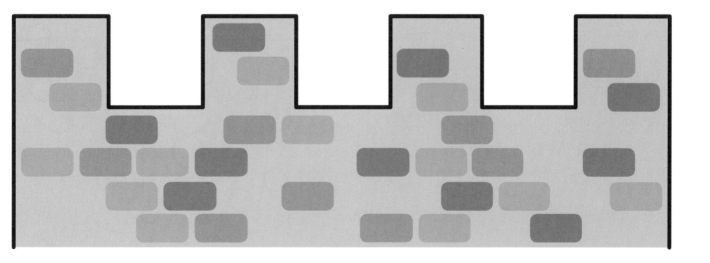

Run your finger around the edge of the round plate. This shape is a circle. A circle has no corners.

Draw wheels on the bicycle.

Colour in this butterfly's round spots.

Squares

Squares have 4 straight sides all the same length. They have 4 corners too. How many squares can you count on the window?

Did you count the window frame too?

How many squares can you find in the picture?

Run your finger around the edge of all the triangles.
A triangle has 3 straight sides and 3 pointed corners.

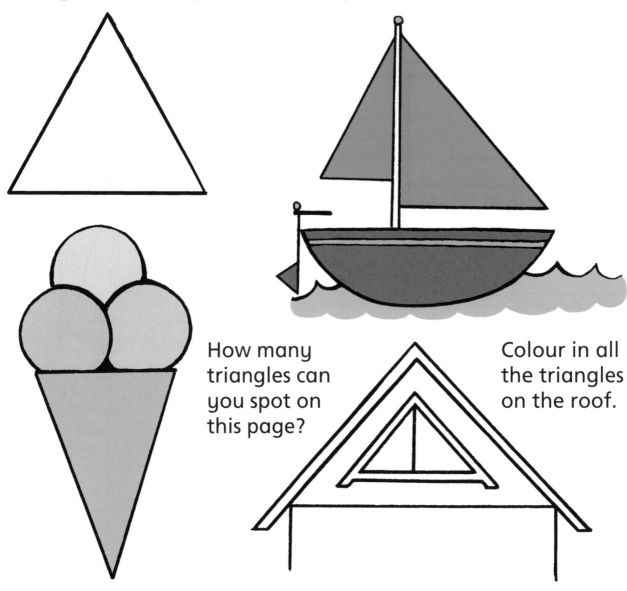

How many triangles can you spot on this page?

Colour in all the triangles on the roof.

Rectangles

Colour in all the rectangles you can see.

How many rectangles can you count on this door?

Large and small

Look carefully at objects
to compare their sizes.

Tick the largest in each group.

More large and small

Join up these sweets in order of size,
starting with the smallest

There are 2 stars of each shape.
Can you spot the shape pairs?

More matching shapes

Which shape does not belong in each set? Talk about your ideas.

Long and short

Which snake is the longest? Which snake is the shortest?

More long and short

Look at these dinosaurs.

Which one has the shortest body?

Which dinosaur has the longest neck?

Up and down

Race to the fire engine!

You will need a dice and two counters.

Go down the poles and up the ladders.

START

To the party

Use 2 counters and a coin.
I person is the tortoise, the other
is the rabbit. Go forward I if you
throw heads, 2 if you throw tails.
The rabbit must pick up another
coin and throw double heads or
tails to go over the hedge. See
who gets to the party first.

stop

How can Mama get to the shop?

Use a counter each. Take turns to throw a dice and count the moves. Choose which way to go around each hole.

Position

Where is Tanto? Choose a word for each of these pictures.

in	out	on	off	up	down

Talk about night and day.

afternoon

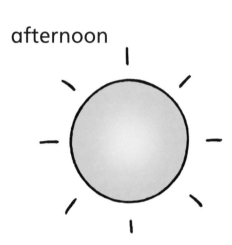

evening

morning

night

Parts of the day

What does Bill do in a day? Put these pictures in order.

Tell the story

Look at the pictures. Tell the story.

Time again

Talk about these pictures. Put them in order.

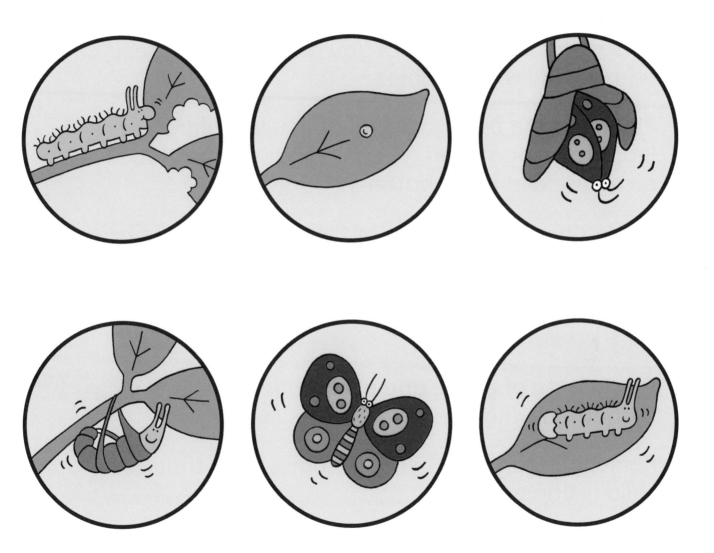

Top tips for learning at home

- Explain that this book and DVD are about shapes and time.

- Choose a time when both you and your child feel relaxed and comfortable.

- Playing is the best way to help young children to learn to enjoy shapes, to talk about sizes and to recognise and make patterns.

- Share the gentle humour of the El Nombre *Numbertime* stories. It is good to laugh!

- Remember that little and often is the best recipe for success.

- Give plenty of praise and encouragement. Learning is about 'having a go'.

- Remember to stop when it becomes clear that your child is tiring.

- Always make sure that learning together is an enjoyable and playful experience!